# How to Become a Successful

# Car Salesman

# By Lamar Eggleston

# Intro

Hello my name is Lamar Eggleston I've been in the car business now for 19 years on all levels from management, the finance manager, and of course a sales person. I would like to start off by saying, this book is designed to go through the steps of how to become a professional car salesman, but before we get there are some key things you need to understand when you make a decision to be a car salesman. <u>Three things you should know.</u>

1. First thing is that you must sell yourself, the vehicle, and the dealership through the experience, so you must look your best, so you can feel your best, and you will perform at your highest levels.
2. The second thing you need to understand is the product you are selling.
3. And the third thing you need to sell is the place you work. That being said I'm not telling you that every place in the world is perfect so the experience is what I'm referring to when I say the place you work.

# Step 1

Step one is called a meet and greet. From the time a customer gets other vehicle or walks up over from your service department you have nine seconds to approach them. Your meet and greet should sound like this welcome to "ABC motors" my name is Lamar and your name is?

It's very important to shake everyone's hand palms up. It's also very important to make sure you have something to write with and your business card. How did the greeting you hand them your business card. This is because most of the time they will forget your name. After that you write their names down. Then you ask if they are here for sales or service. When they see sales you didn't say are you looking for new or preowned. Then you ask if they're interested in a car, truck or SUV.

# Step 2

Step two is selection. The goal here is to find one car one color in stock or locate to do business today or in the future that is the definition of the term "the pick" in the car business. Once that is completed you do a walk around or walk around is a feature benefit presentation of the exterior and interior of the vehicle. When you mention a feature you stay its benefit for example this vehicle is equipped with a 60/40 split folding rear seat is the feature the benefit for more storage. You give for exterior feature benefit.

On your walk to the front or rear of the vehicle and state the vehicles warranty. Your walk around should end up on the passenger side of the vehicle every time at this point you open the door and ask the customer  to have a seat in the vehicle. During your selection walk around presentation it's important to find out what the most important features are to the vehicle this is how you engage your walk around. For example if a customer says what got them interested in the vehicle was it safety features you're going to customize your walk around emphasizing on safety features. Now back to where we left off. When you're sitting in the vehicle the same rules apply, make sure you know every single button on the dash in a feature benefit format. You don't have to cover all of them just the very significant ones to this customer. Any service such as one star or XM satellite radio you give a presentation not a feature benefit.

Once you were done going over the vehicle you ask the customer if there are any questions. Any complement given to the car from the customer you repeat back to them in a question form in such as, Wow this vehicle really does look and read. You would repeat back to them it does look good in red doesn't it. The more times the customer says yes to you the smoother the close will go later on in time.

# Step 3

Now step three the demo ride. The sales consultant always drives first always making right turns this is so you never passed through oncoming traffic. At your dealership designated switch point he then put the car in park and say it's your turn to drive us back. During this demo read you do establish who the primary driver is. You do ask if anyone else is going to be driving the vehicle. You do ask if the vehicle is going to for personal or business use. Important note if two people are going to be making a decision you do have to switch points where you asked the other individual to drive if they're available. This is also time to get to know your customer you ask about what they do for a living if they retired you ask them what they do for a living. You do give a brief explanation of yourself and some personal facts about you. Such as I saw the United States Air Force, I went to Penn State University. Things like that.

Once you're back at the dealership ask a customer questions to help build up your number, when I say your number, I mean on a scale of 1 to 10 how did they read the vehicle. For example you say to the customer you told me you enjoyed the ride, you also said you like color, and the gas mileage was great. So based on all these things you rate the vehicle a ten, Right! If the answer is NO it's a 7 you ask what they would change to make it a 10 they say the price, you say Oh I get it, if the deal was right it would be a 10. If the customer says they didn't like the size or it didn't have enough power, you are not done selling you need to keep selling repeating the selection and demo until you arrive at the "pick". Once you do. Then you move to the next part of the sell.

# Step 4

Step four is dealership presentation. In the step you do a feature benefit presentation of the benefits of buying a car from whatever dealership you work for and also the features and benefits of our service department. Take the customer to your service department give them the business cards of your service writer service manager and also your parts manager. Explain the benefits of your rental cars, or shuttle services. You explain the convenience of your service hours. This is the second portion of what you need to do to sell yourself the vehicle and the place you work.

# Step 5

Step five is presentation of the numbers. You asked
the customer if we can make a deal make sense to you
today can we are in your business today. Don't get
discouraged if the customer tells you no. This
happens a lot but remember the definition of a pick,
is one car, one color in stock or location to do
business today or in the future. This is important to
remember because just because you didn't sell them a
car today does not mean you will not sell them a car.
So when you go to your manager you have to have some
type of timeline of when the customer would like to
do business that time like maybe a week, a day, and
next spring. It doesn't matter what the timeline is
we just need to know what it is. Trust me, anyone in
your management team will try to move forward sooner
than the timeline of the customer that's what we do
in this business.

# Step 6

Step six is about the trade, as a salesperson we need
to go out to the trade if they have one. Ask how many
miles are on tires, if there is any damage ask them
if they are trading it in that condition, if they got
any estimate on fixing the damage, go for a ride in
there trade with them so you can see how well the
breaks work, if all the windows work if the air blows
cold or heat turns on. If it has 4x4 works if any
warning lights are on the dash. Ask if the vehicle
has and warranty left or if they purchased and
extended one. If there is a pay-off or if they have
the title. If there is a pay-off call the bank and
get the 20 day pay-off.

# Step 7

Step seven go to your manager with all the pieces to
the deal, the pick, the timeline of business, the
trade information. Make sure you tell him they when
to service and that you went on your demo and your
scale of 1-10 number.

# Step 8

Step eight present your first set of numbers to your
customer, starting with the down money from customer
than the payments, than the selling price minus the
trade, plus the pay-off and then the difference. Once
you say this you hand the pen to the customer and ask
them to circle which payment works best for them. In
a perfect world they circle one. This doesn't happen,
so when they don't take the pen you ask them if there
is an issue and then the issue comes out. Don't panic
this is normal. In a perfect world you can get the
offer from what they want. This can be a challenging
time in the process.

# Step 9

The ninth step is the close, most of the time this can be done with you, but there will be times that a manger has to get involved to do this part of the deal. This could mean justifying a lower amount for a trade, explaining why the payment is higher, or it could mean they have extend the terms. A number of things could be involved in the close.

# Step 10

Last step is delivery this is important to make sure
you have the car clean; make sure you go over the
vehicle again you make sure all the money down is
receipted. You make sure all documents are signed.
Make sure the trade paperwork is down correctly and
most importantly ask for referrals.

# The Facts

Now everything I talked about doesn't happen in that exact order all the time but it is important to remember if you want a high level of success you must do the steps. And you will be successful 95% of the time!

I've just taken you through the steps of the sale however there are other important things that you must know to be a successful sales person. Number one is prospecting not only the customers you sell but any manifest list or any type of lead sources or any type of material that your dealership provides to you that you can call, email and text every single day. This may require some level of Phone training.

# Deep Dive

Now we dove into the 10 basic steps to becoming a professional sales person however now we need to talk about the two pieces to the car deal. The first portion of the car deal is selling the car because you're selling your feet and your closing your seat, what that means is after you do a meet and greet presentation a demo ride, and a presentation of your dealership. You confirm that that's the car they want to buy with the closing questions. You must get a confirmation or you didn't lock down that deal. Now the selling portion of the car deal is complete. The second part of the deal is working the car deal now let's not be confused working the car deal is not the same as selling the car, the trade, the payment the down payment, all those are pieces of working the car deal so that it ultimately ends up in completing the transaction.

The first thing I would like to start with is identifying the trade the trade is a controversial piece of the deal because most people have an opinion based upon some small bit of research of what they believe their trade is worth whether right or wrong it is what they believe. When a customer makes an offer to you on your trade it sounds like this. Well, I think my car is worth X-amount of dollars. You politely ask him. How did you arrive at that number? You will be shocked to hear some sort of Internet information nonsense, most of the time its Kelley blue book.

If this is the situation you say I understand Kelly is a well-respected resource for a third-party suggestion of what a trade could be worth, now you then say. Can we do it together? You asked a customer if you and them can sit there and do a Kelley blue book together in doing so you also go out to the lot with the customer and go over the car with the customer asking such questions as how many miles are on your tires are you going to trade this vehicle in for in the current condition of which it sits right now these are very punctual questions because everything that you say you can document in the report that you pull from Kelly's research. This report you will bring to your manager when it comes time to talk about the figures.

The most important piece of the car deal to the customer is where the monthly payment falls the reason is because most people do not have the ability to pay for a car 100% so it's important to identify that. How you do that is when they say I want to talk about the price I want to talk about the price I want to talk about this I will talk about that well Mr. Customer I understand that is how much of a percentage you are  paying for this car in cash the rest of it will have to come out of the banks and they will say what are you willing to put down $1000 Dollars or 2000 or 3000 it doesn't matter because of the amount of money that we're trying to purchase usually exceeds a larger figure it doesn't really matter how much money they're putting down. The majority of the purchase will come from a standpoint of borrowing it from a bank. So the question is OK I understand what you're saying Mr. Customer what you're telling me is you want to borrow most of the money from the bank correct. They will say yes you say back to them well it sounds like to me we need to find something that fits within your monthly budget.

Once a customer agrees to what you're saying based off the fact that you just put in front of them you now have the ability to talk to them on an even playing field not ignoring but it knowledge and only that the payment is the most important part of the conversation not the trade not the price not anything but what is affordable to the customer at the Pacific point in time no not saying that every customer is willing to go to that point of the field most of them will see what I just want to know what the overall prices and you keep stating to them, I understand what you're saying to us So what you're saying Mr. Customer what you're saying is at $19,047.22 you're purchasing this car no matter what if the payment is $1100 a month you're at peace with that as long as that price point exist is that what you're saying 99% of the time the answer to the question is going to be absolutely not I need to make sure it fits within my budget again driving home the point that the budget is the biggest portion of the car deal.

Now most people make the decisions on their budget
based upon a few things the first one is what the
previous payment was even if the car is five years
old, it doesn't matter if they don't want to pay more
than what they're currently paying. The second one is
based upon what they saw on an ad. So the words you
say to the customer is here is what it cost to
purchase this vehicle not what do you want to pay for
it but this is the price of ownership although it may
sound like simple math that a $30,000 vehicle does
not come out to 250 a month customers still believe
in the miracle.

So educating the customer is not a bad thing it's a reality if the customer really can't pay more than a dollar figure that they are talking about then you're going to have to make some adjustments on the side of the deal. It's important to remember that the words. If I can would you buy it right now is not a reality he's trying to convert a customer into a buyer but using false pretense instead you asked questions like this Mr. customer no matter what it is you purchase your budget will not and cannot exceed $300, am I stating that correctly.

Now once you bring the second option to the customers table one of two things will happen and they were either move them self-up in monthly budget or they will settle for something less this is the reality. As I said earlier I don't want you to read this and think that every word and situation is every situation but the important part to remember is that I am touching on the everyday most common ones. Let's talk more about timelines. Customer believe that if they tell you that they are ready that day instead of saying a couple of weeks or months, that pressure will be put on them. The reality of this is, they are correct! That's why they give all the excuses in the world. So as a sales professional is important to not forget the goal, the pick doesn't mean today but it does mean when it's time to make it happen it happens with you.

Another very important part of being the best is practice, always remember that training isn't above anyone in the company. All owners, all managers, all sales. This is how you stay ahead of trends the technology all the different parts of this business. I told you I the title of this book I was going to teach you how to become a professional salesperson. The first thing that must be addressed before anyone calls himself a professional at anything you must define what makes you a professional. Well, it's easy. Ask yourself have I made professional grade money for this job, if you need an example, if someone told they were a professional football player, you know what kind of income they are referring too. So for our business 100k a year is the benchmark. At least in the northeast part of Pennsylvania.

Earlier I spoke about phones. Today's sales people depend on business Development Coordinator people to set the tempo for appointments. The reality is a professionals only needs their own efforts to calculate their income not a phone person. The purpose of a phone call or text or email is set the appointment. The key to take from this is, never stop dialing, I mean never! It is one of the biggest power keys in the world of sales! Another key to the profession is what I would consider a lost art form called prospecting. This is about asking your customers, friends and family for referrals and making yourself look for old business that you thought was lost. Remember new business, bringing your card with you everywhere, making sure you engage your social media with pictures and tagging all your customers sharing your business with everyone you come in contact with will only benefit you.

Written By Lamar J Eggleston

Copyright 2020


Vincent A Eggleston Jr. Publishing